# For All That Brought You Here

To _______________________________

For All That Brought You Here

# JASMINES IN HER HAIR

POETRY FOR THE SOUL

KALPESH DESAI

# THE JOURNEY

*Those three little words that mean a lot*
*Aren't "I Love You",*
*They are "No Matter What".*
*~ Kalpesh Desai ~*

# FOREWORD

Everybody has a poet in them. If everything exists inside of language, then it is the love of language that makes loving that much more exciting.

I have been writing since a very young age and I have compiled a selection of my romantic poems that delve into the distinctions that have come my way through my journey through love, loss, pain, reconciliation and finding love again.

I have realized that every relationship can be treasured, and that there is as much relief in releasing ourselves from our past, as there is in finding someone who gives our ability to love a new lease of life.

This book is a journey from the first throes of passion, to when one finds their way to the soulmate they have been waiting for their entire life. I pray that *Jasmines In Her Hair* serves not just as a reminder but also an avenue to find access to what love looks, feels, and sounds like in the mind of a poet.

I do hope you will read this labor of love and I would love to read about your feedback in the reviews of this book. Do follow me on Instagram (@kalpeshdesai.official) where I release spoken word versions of my poetry, from time to time.

Lots of love,

# PRELUDE

# UNSPOKEN DESIRES

Sometimes I wonder
if I could linger,
gaze at you a little longer,
as these feelings grow stronger,
while droplets trace their path
across all that I crave.

I pray that your divinity
longs for the same affinity
I seek—
with my body, mind, and soul.
My thoughts spin out of control,
and I wonder
if holding that hand
would pull me asunder.

And still I wonder—
can I silence what stirs inside,
when I glimpse, for a fleeting second,
what the angel tries to hide?

# SLUMBER

When you sense
my breath upon your neck,
in the depths of slumber,
know that I am a wreck.

In these dreams of you,
where my senses run riot,
I wonder—
do you dream too,
of how you are the storm
to my quiet?

# SAFE HAVEN

What is seduction,
if not love,
born at the sacred junction
where safe haven is craved?

# MINE

---

Nibble at her ear,
draw her near.
Bite the nape of her neck,
hold the passion in check.

Explore every crest and mound,
hush her sound.

And when it begins to flow—
the rhythm, the rhyme—
we will know.

I will be hers.
She will be mine.

# ADDICTION

Would you let me set you on fire,
bring you to the cusp of desire?

Make love to you till morning comes,
engulf you, as if we are one.

Will there be sweet surrender
to this addiction
that keeps pulling me under?

# THE MANY WAYS I LOVE YOU

I will go down on you,
my tongue exploring
every inch of you.

And when my lips meet yours,
my tongue inside,
my eyes locked with yours,
I will mouth, *"I love you,"*
whispering it again and again
until you call my name aloud,
your sweet moans
echoing in the chambers of my heart.

And then, you pull me up,
guiding me in…
to you.

# THERE'S SOMETHING ABOUT YOU

There's something about you
that makes me want to hold you tight,
to lose myself in your eyes,
to wrap you in my arms,
and fill your days with light.

I don't know how long
I've felt this way,
or where this path may lead—
I cannot say.
But when the walls crumble and fall,
and a flower dares to grow,
I'll brush away the rubble of the past,
so that love may finally show.

# LOVE LANGUAGE

Eat me with your words,
caress me with your thoughts.
Let your eyes be the cords
that tie my soul in knots.

# YOUNG LOVE

We had just crossed
the age of consent,
never knowing
what true love meant.

We made promises we couldn't keep,
tried to soar before we could leap.
And now, as the years drift by,
we've built these walls—
wide and high.

We have crossed the age of regret,
placing memories on the mantle,
lest we forget.
And when we think of
what could have been,
we wonder why
we never wiped the slate clean.

# SHIPS IN THE NIGHT

If we are meant to cross paths,
we will.

And yet, you've brushed past me
a thousand times,
with barely a glance.

But when the moment arrives,
when time stands still,
don't be a ship in the night,
leaving fate to chance.

# TAKE MY NAME

When I hear my name
whispered in your voice,
a thousand cells
ignite in flames,
and every inch of my being
rejoices.

What are the depths of desire
that we seek,
when we dance on this pyre
where tender hearts
dare not speak?

Consume me in a million ways,
until nothing remains but love.
And when you do,
meet my gaze,
so I may be
all that you dream of.

# ANGEL

And I gaze
at her reflection—
an apsara,
veiled in steam and haze,
droplets tracing perfection.

My thoughts torn
between desire and need,
my eyes betray inhibitions freed,
blood rushing
where passions lead.

Is it wrong to say
that I want it all?
Will she cast away
her fears at my call?

And in this moment,
in the here and now,
does she sense
that she is mine—
somehow?

# LILITH

Can't you see
what you're doing to me?
My thoughts in ruins,
my mind in turmoil,
and this heart—
torn apart.

# BETWEEN LINES AND ELEMENTS

What if love
was nothing but the space
between phrases?

Lines that make us smile,
keeping our hearts warm for a while.

What if we exist in physics,
but it is chemistry
that makes it real?

# UNSPOKEN LOVE

In how many ways
do I love thee?
If only you knew,
if only you could see
these feelings for you.

So far away, so far apart,
so much to learn—
and yet,
she holds my heart.

# FRENZY

A love so naughty,
thoughts
that will not let us be.

Rough palms
trace her slender neck,
frenzied bodies—
and yet,

a passion
held in check.

# GUILTY PLEASURES

You and I
speak till the break of dawn,
a guilty pleasure
veiling souls lovelorn.

And so we tuck away
these secrets,
into hearts forlorn.

# DINNER

When we make love,
you don't call my name,
and yet, I hear you loud and clear.

When I devour you,
your demons, I tame—
my lips searing
every edge of your frame.

And if they see
the wanton lust in our eyes,
there'll be no difference
between you and I.

# BREAKFAST

I wake up to this vision of you,
your hips facing me,
like they already knew.

My lips explore the nape of your neck,
blood rushing south,
my mind an absolute wreck.

I move my way up to nibble your ear,
whispering promises of the things
you want to feel and hear.

You tease me with your delicate curves,
while I'm breathing heavy,
trying to calm my nerves.

I hold you down as I go down on you,
warm, wet, and sweet,
telling me that you want it
as much as I do.

My rough hands caress your delicate skin,
that look of surprise as I slip myself in.
Your moans echo in my head,
syncing to the rhythm of the bed.

And when we are spent and finish up strong,
we wonder how something so right
could feel so wrong.

# WHEN YOU WAKE UP

I want to wake up
and find you
snuggled deep into me.

I want you to see,
the moment you open your eyes,
how gently
I move a strand of hair
away from your cheek.

I want you to feel
the love in my touch—
the way my lips meet yours
as I turn you toward me.

I want you to hear
how every heartbeat of mine
rhymes with your name.

I want you to smell
the lingering fragrance
on our bodies—
reminders of the night before.

And I want you to know
that as long as
we're engulfed in these feelings,
this will always be love.

# SHUT EYE

Every night, as the moon adorns the sky,
navigating thoughts as the hours pass by,
I wonder if you can hear my heart's lullaby—

moist lips letting kisses fly,
sweet nothings mouthed by throats so dry,
awaiting moments
when we can hold each other's sighs,
where the stars strain to find you and I.

# IS IT TOO SOON?

Sometimes,
I wake up at night,
thinking of the ways
I would hold you—
so tight,
like I never want to let go,
snuggling you
like there's no tomorrow.

And when you ask,
"Isn't it too soon?"
I reply…
"Isn't our love
as old as the moon?"

# WHEN YOU TAKE MY NAME

Every time you say my name,
you set every fiber
of my being aflame.

Do you know what that means?
That I am the moth,
that your fire redeems.

# YESTERDAY'S EMBERS

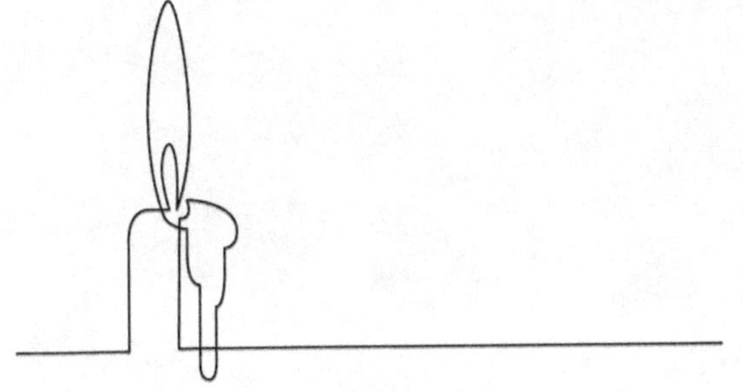

# YOU HAD ME AT THAT SMILE

You had me at that smile.
You lost me
when you gave up on that last mile.

# WILL THERE BE ONE MORE OF YOU?

Will there be one more of you?
Can it exist in someone new?

# JUST BECAUSE

Just because I couldn't show it,
doesn't mean I didn't care.

Just because you couldn't see it,
doesn't mean I wasn't there.

Just because I let go of it,
doesn't mean I didn't want to share.

Just because I could stitch it,
doesn't mean it didn't tear.

Just because we couldn't fix it,
doesn't mean it was beyond repair.

Just because we can no longer have it,
doesn't mean you aren't in my prayers.

# I DIDN'T LOVE YOU

I didn't love you—
at least, not in the way
you wanted me to.

I didn't care—
at least, not in the way
you needed my heart laid bare.

I didn't listen—
at least, not in the way
that made my eyes glisten.

I didn't touch—
at least, not in the way
you longed for so much.

I didn't know then
I wouldn't have those chances again.

I didn't know then
you can't rewind time
to way back when.

# I'VE RUN OUT OF ALIBIS

For all the promises unkept,
for the moments
I wasn't present,

for all the tears you wept,
for the truths
left unpleasant—

I've run out of alibis.

And perhaps forever is a fantasy,
but when I close my eyes,
you're all that I can see.

# FIND ME IN YOUR PHOTOGRAPHS

I'll visit you again someday,
in memories that still hold sway.

You'll find me in your photographs,
reminding you of our smiles,
reliving our laughs.

Remember me when the day is done,
when the moon reminds you
of the nights
when we were one.

Remember how I used to call your name,
on days we were spent of blame.

And the moments we shared, however insane,
will no longer be masked in pain.

Because when it was time to leave,
we chose to let go—and forgive.

# THE VOID

Perhaps
the emptiness you feel when it's over
is nothing but space—
to newly seek and discover.

# THE WEIGHT YOU CARRY

Perhaps the weight you carry
is on your mind, not your shoulder.

Perhaps you wouldn't be so weary
if you realized—it's a pebble,
not a boulder.

# CAN I LOVE YOU A LITTLE LESS?

I know I never said this before,
but is it okay
if I love you a little less
and love me a little more?

# MAYBE

Maybe I couldn't love you
the way you wanted me to.

Maybe you never loved me
enough—
to let me be.

# SYNTHETIC EMBRACE

What secrets do you hide,
behind those lovely eyes?
Who will show up
from deep inside,
when laid bare are these ugly lies?

Will I see two of you,
when I gaze upon your face,
suffocating in your synthetic embrace?

Will you then see,
'twas about you.
'Twas never about me?

# MAYBE, I AM NOT TOO MUCH

Maybe, I'm not too much.
Maybe you've just been
used to too little.

Much like those
who walk with a crutch,
find the ground too fickle.

# SETTING YOUR HEART AFLAME

Do you remember me,
or has the sound of my name
ceased to be
words that set your heart aflame?

# REMEMBER THE UNSAID

We remember all
that remained unsaid,
in the darkest corners
of our head.

Hold me in your memories,
so that you may remember
all our stories.

# BEREFT

It was the night before I left
that I already knew—
love was bereft.

And so we let go
of all we had hoped and desired—
dreams unfulfilled, souls tired.

We released ourselves
from the hurtful words
that haunted our ears,
the ones that left us
shedding silent tears.

# DUST

Those distant memories
of guileless trust,
lay buried by time,
beneath a once forever love's
ashes and dust.

# WEAK PROMISES

The weakest promises
are often made
when difficult conversations
are the ones they wish to evade.

# REMEMBER THIS

When all feels amiss,
remember this—
our first stolen kiss.

# BROKEN PROMISES

As much as these broken promises
couldn't find their way,
I can still see your face—
as clear as day.

# NEVER ENOUGH

Maybe I should have told you
that I loved you—because I do.

Maybe I should have held you
when you needed me to.

Maybe I should have been present,
to show you what I meant.

Maybe I should have turned my head,
to hear what was left unsaid.

And maybe I was always there,
in my own way,
expressing my love and care.

# SEASONS

Nothing spells fall
like fallen leaves
in their tapestried splendor,
soon to be forgotten,
as if they never mattered at all.

Much like the memories of us,
to her.

The changing seasons
beckon the close of a chapter,
one where we were bereft of reasons.

And like the long nights,
we wonder—
what comes after?

# WISH UPON A STAR

I know you once wished
upon a shooting star,
and I had promised
it would be all right in the end.

And see—
we've come so very far,
with limitless love
and hearts to mend.

# SMOKE AND MIRRORS

And the moment it broke,
I realized—
it was all mirrors and smoke.

I picked up the pieces
of shattered dreams,
stitched the patches
where it tore at the seams.

And now, scabs have formed
where scars once stood.
Dead skin—
easily removed.

# THE TUNE IN MY HEAD

"I'm sorry, we are out of tune,"
she said.

Then why are you
the only song
stuck in my head?

# I DON'T MISS YOU

I don't miss your touch,
or your kisses, that much.

I don't miss your voice at all,
or the sound of your footfall.

I don't miss the sparkle in your eye,
or the silent tears when you cry.

I don't miss your freshly bathed fragrance,
your hair tangled in innocence.

I don't miss you chiding me,
or the way you used to let me be.

I don't miss your laughter,
nor the way we spooned the morning after.

I don't miss you—

but then again, I lie.
With these words,
your absence I justify.

# SETTING YOU FREE

I think of you often
on nights like these,
when your touch would soften
my thoughts
and put my demons at ease.

Now the clouds shroud the moon,
much like your memories of me.

I wonder—
did I let go too soon?
I wonder—
did leaving me set you free?

# WE STOOD HERE ONCE

The place where I stand,
waiting for you,
is where we once stood, too.

That moon, gazing down upon me,
perhaps seeks you out, too,
across the sea.

And it's nights like these
that remind me of broken promises,
sealed with our first kiss.

# UNWRITTEN BOOKS

And I saw her standing there,
the wind playing games
with her hair.

Her eyes gazed into the distance,
dreaming a dream into existence.

We glanced at each other and smiled,
seeing the pain we tried so hard to hide.

Though no words were spoken that day,
we heard the stories we had to say.

Held back by the fear of being twice bitten,
another book was left unwritten.

# BY THE TIME I WAS READY

You said we could grow old together,
but I wasn't sure.

By the time I was ready,
you weren't here.

# IT IS WINTER

It is winter,
and you're not here.

It wasn't about me.
It wasn't about her.

# MIND OVER MATTER

She did not mind.
He did not matter.

And there it was—
mind over matter.

# WRITTEN IN METAPHORS,
## RELEASED IN RHYMES

She lives on in my rhymes,
hidden in metaphors—
memories of bygone times,

when I was once hers,
and she was forever mine.

# LYRICS OF LIFE

I'll write words left unspoken,
of a spirit still unbroken.

I'll write of all that's amiss,
memoirs of a forgotten kiss.

I'll write of loss, of pain, of sorrow—
a promise of a brighter tomorrow.

For these are the lyrics of life,
the song I sing when times are rife.

# FORBIDDEN FRUIT

Taken
Forbidden fruit
A love forsaken
Lost in her pursuit
Broken

# IN ANOTHER LIFE

Long conversations,
kindred souls entwine,
love expressed in silent invocations,
while worlds apart.

Words unsaid,
walls around the heart,
a poem unfinished—
not for want of reason or rhyme.

The promise of completion
resides in another lifetime.

# AMBER

Unspoken
Unshed tears
These suppressed fears
Fossilized in heart's chamber
Amber

# MADE A MEMORY OUT OF THIS

They stood side by side,
after a long journey together.

Looking back at all they had amassed,
and all that was amiss—

and yet,
they made a memory of this.

# I WANTED TO LEAVE SOMETHING BEHIND

I was faulted for all I couldn't say,
but it was in silence,
that I found my way.

I was faulted
for not walking away from the fight,
but I couldn't hang up my gloves
until I made it right.

And then, I was faulted
for the time I could not find,
when all I wanted
was to leave something behind.

# DID WE JUST LET THEM WIN?

Did we just let them win?
Punishing ourselves
for words we had left unsaid.

The only sin
was letting them
mess with our head.

# DEVOID OF BLAME

And if they wish to say goodbye,
hold them close to your chest,
and wipe the tear from their eye.

Say their name,
just as you did before,
when days were devoid of blame.

Let them know
you'll visit them again someday,
in memories that linger
and forever hold sway.

That they can find you in photographs,
whenever they wish
to remember those smiles
and relive those laughs.

Most of all, remind them—
that when it's time to leave,

you can choose to let go
and forgive.

And then, all those moments you've shared,
however insane,
will no longer be masked in pain.

# THE SWEETEST GOODBYE

When you knew
that it wasn't anger, but love,
and you sensed words
unspoken and unheard.

When her grace
was all you could think of,
when you remembered
the moments endeared.

When you knew
there was a tear in her eye,
You knew then—
it was the sweetest goodbye.

# TREASURE

Those distant memories
of you and me—
hazy dreams, distorted by reality.

A home we built, brick by brick,
on promises of togetherness
through thin and thick.

And what was one is now split in two,
time would take its toll—who knew?

When the walls began to crack,
it didn't matter
who first turned their back.

And though we are no longer together,
it's the ballad of you and I
that I treasure.

# IT IS WHAT IT IS

It is what it is.
Nothing more, nothing less.

No credit. No blame.
Not hers, nor his.

# RESILIENCE

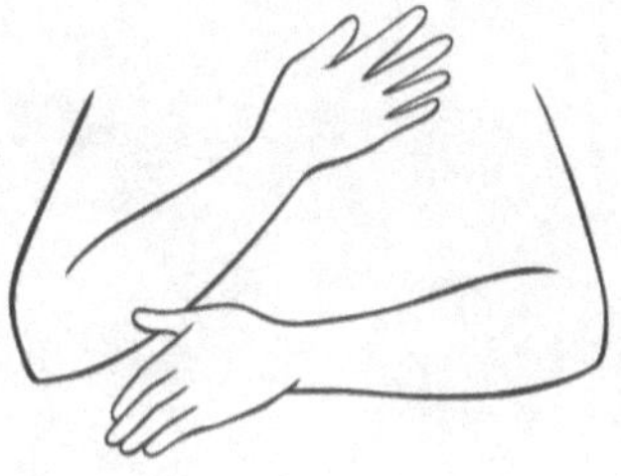

# CONSUMPTION

*We fear all that can consume us.*
*Disease,*
*Death,*
*Deluge,*
*Fire,*
*Love,*
*Us.*

# DEBRIS

Come, lay your head
upon my shoulder,
where your thoughts of dread
shall disappear.

These arms will shield you,
keeping at bay
the malevolent storms
of the past that pursue.

Close your eyes,
hold on to me,
so you may finally say goodbye
to your soul's debris.

# WHAT COMES AFTER

'Twas that kind of night—
tears, upsets,
make-up love after a fight.

And what better way
to show her that you love her
than this—
sealing every argument
with a kiss?

# SELF-LOVE

I saw what you did there,
but I loved myself too much to care.

# NOT WHO, BUT WHAT

Perhaps, if we focused less
on who caused the pain,
and more on what,
maybe then,
it wouldn't happen again.

# LETTING GO

Perhaps,
The endings we hold on to
do not allow us to grasp something new.

# SAVE ME FROM ME

From the fates that won't let me be,
from all that was written in my destiny.

From the maps I follow
and the sights I can't unsee,
from the voices in my head
that refuse to sync in symphony.

From the haunt of nightmares
born of distant memory—
the only way to break free
is to save me, from me.

# DARKNESS

You'll find that darkness
was never the absence of light—
but a shield,
a cover to win every fight.

# HOT KNIVES

And those hurtful words you utter
cut through my heart,
like a hot knife through butter.

# WALKING IN THE RAIN

I am sentimental,
so I walk in the rain,
shedding tears
to hide my pain.

And though I cannot
unbreak my heart,
I can piece it together,
part by part.

# IT WAS TIME

It was time
to let go.
It wasn't mine—
I told myself so.

And someday, you will see,
it wasn't about you—
it was about me.

We existed in conversations
we never had before.
I had loved myself less
to love you more.

# SILENT BATTLES

I lay on my bed,
eyes open wide,
thoughts churning in my head,
as I toss from side to side.

Haunted by the things
I could have—
or shouldn't have—done.
Secrets I'll carry to my grave,
silent battles I had won,
and moments
when I hadn't been so brave.

I dream of summers past
and wonder how many seasons remain.
I know I must break the mold
in which the die was cast,
to be absolved of pride,
ego, guilt, and pain.

# IN BETWEEN MAYBES

When times are strange, and people too,
when relationships change—
is there nothing you can do?

The dreams that drove you once—,
do they keep you awake still?
Are you still one who hunts,
or have you lost your will?

The ones you've loved and lost—
how do you remember them?
Do you now see the cost
of the words that tore the hem?

In the cloak of those beliefs
to which you once inclined,
was truth ever a release,
or did you leave it all behind?

Do we yearn to be free,
yet hold on to chains,
straining to see
beyond our regrets and pains?

Will you stand alone
once you reach the top?
Tired of making it on your own—
a journey with no pit stop.

Hurry up.
You know we don't have time.
Fill that cup—
we've got mountains to climb.

# I RAISE MY GLASS TO ANOTHER YEAR

I raise my glass to another year,
no flights of fancy, no delusions, no fear.
It takes a moment to recognize
that face in the mirror,
blurry-eyed, and yet a vision clear.

Graying temples, crow's feet around the eyes,
weather-beaten hands—
tell-tale signs of the wise.
No longer indestructible in body and soul,
a boy that's turned into a man that's whole.

Forgiveness comes easy,
I've learned to let it be.
Determination ingrained, energy a skill,
have I reached my pinnacle?
I doubt I ever will!

I revere those who've held me,
the bonds that tied, and ones I've set free.
I've walked down life's highway,
made a difference, and found my way.
I have my sights on what I'm looking for,
I'll steady my pace; I'll be ready for more.

Grateful to those who put in their lot
to build a life's dream.
A prayer for those who chose to step back,
in the fear that the ship would lose steam.

Looking back at a time that's past,
lives that I have touched, loved, or lost.
Doors once open, now bolted fast,
or bridges burnt, that I'd once crossed.

I've got the sun in my eye, and the wind on my face,
every challenge shall be countered,
every opportunity I shall embrace.

I am now the beacon and the shore,
I've caught my breath, and ready for more!

Every milestone achieved,
will be a goal fulfilled,
Every bridge crossed,
will be one that I will build.

# WHEN THE NIGHT CREEPS IN

I draw on my last cigarette,
like I did my last regret.

The night is creeping in,
calling out the demons within.

An unmet expectation, an unfulfilled dream,
unexplored paths, or an action extreme.

I choose to stifle their screams and sighs,
push them aside, and shut my eyes.

There will always be the break of dawn,
signaling a time to move on.

# ON YOUR CASE

When the world comes at you,
with brickbats and words untrue,
with judgments and accusations,
advice and unmet expectations—

sift through the noise,
maintain your poise.

They can't break your iron will,
if you can keep your mind still.

And trust
that you can craft new realities
out of dust.

# WHAT WE DESERVED

It's not *what you deserve*, that you get,
It's what you're willing to accept.

# UNREAD

I did not ask, and she did not say.
And so, that unread book was cast away.

# HAPPINESS, A MYTH

And our soul seeks
that which we don't have.
We taint our skies with golden streaks,
only to see our dreams cut down in half.

And just when we begin to believe
that happiness is a myth,
comes the light—
beckoning the dark to leave,

showing you
that you were all
you needed to begin with.

# TIREDNESS

I'm tired.
Tired of keeping up pretenses
and lowering my defenses.

I'm tired of faking a smile,
of always walking that extra mile.
I'm tired of trying to be
your best version of me.

Today, I will rest awhile,
for I refuse to be on trial.

Today, I'll take time out for me,
set my mind at ease, and set my spirit free.
Your validation, I shall no longer crave,
nor bury my aspirations in a grave.

Today, I've decided—
no longer shall I remain tired,
nor let go of what I once desired.

# EGO

We built it wide and tall,
on what we thought
were foundations strong.

But we didn't know it would fall,
weakened by the war
between right and wrong.

We sought True North
on the compasses we held,
ignoring maps
laid down by men wiser and greater.

Wisdom and insight were soon quelled
when our ego
was declared the victor.

# BOOKENDS

You and I hurt in silence,
sitting apart, like bookends.

Heavy thoughts loom,
and like clouds, they strain—
to fall, as words often do,
like the rain.

# WE BURIED LOVE HERE

You did not seek to ask,
and I chose not to answer.

And so we gaze
into the depths of that silence,
because we buried love here.

# I DON'T LIVE THERE ANYMORE

You came looking for me
in the dark places
where you thought I'd be.

I just thought I'd let you know—
I don't live there anymore.

# MY JOURNEY

I've traveled many a mile,
made pit stops between
each tear and smile.

At every crossroad,
when it seemed a bit too much,
I shifted my paradigm—
without a clutch.

When they came at me,
fueling doubt and fear,
I blazed through those roadblocks—
on high gear.

I've never been one
to deny my mistakes.
I've learned when to stop
and hit the brakes.

For the times I've been misunderstood,
I've taken the blame—
when I could.

I do not regret
what was broken or not built.
I do not intend
on feeding my guilt.

I own every dent,
every scratch, every flaw.
I hold my tongue—
I won't be quick to the draw.

And when I set out
to do something new,
I'll take a moment
to glance at my rear view.

I no longer crave
their validation or praise.
I can look in the mirror
and meet my gaze.

I stand now,
strong and tall,
not shy of owning it all.

Don't judge my journey—
you've got no right,
unless you've been by my side,
fighting my fight.

# SPLINTERED MEMORIES

In the dark recesses of my mind,
tucked away safely,
are splintered memories
of times unkind—
and all those who tried to break me.

Shards I've walked over
and left behind,
broken shackles
from which I've set myself free.

# THE DISTANCE BETWEEN US

The distance that separates us
can be measured
by the footfall
of unnecessary words.

# WE GET ONLY AS MUCH AS WE PUT IN

We spoke so much,
but we did not listen.
We craved each other,
yet did not touch.

We saw,
but were blind to what was missing.
We limped,
but never asked for a crutch.

And then we found
that we could receive back
only as much as we put in.

# WEATHERED

You see me now,
weathered and worn—
a man, where once stood a boy,
wondering how

he could love,
and yet leave,
with his spirit untorn.

# I OFFER MY RESISTANCE

I've built, I've broken,
buried deep, grief unspoken.

I've loved and lost,
burnt bridges that I've crossed.

And I've grown, I've changed,
learned to love those estranged.

I refuse to call this a cursed existence.
Give me strife, and I'll offer my resistance.

# REDISCOVERY

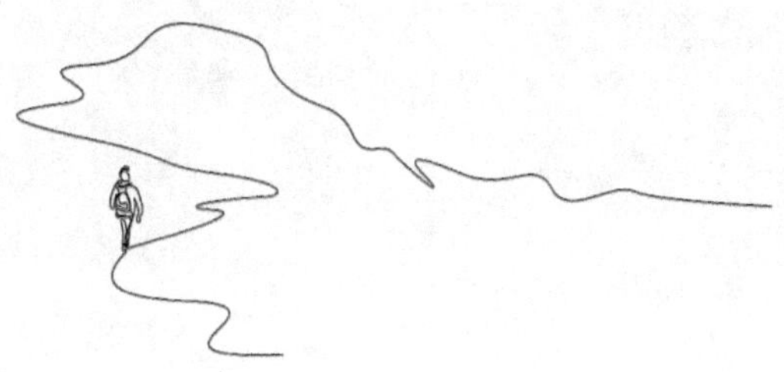

# TRUST

Here I am—
vulnerable,
afraid to trust,

wondering...
would you, too,
betray, turning promises to dust?

Or will you be the one
to show me
that I can bare who I am—

without being judged,
without being misunderstood,

and in the comfort of your warmth...
simply be me?

# SURRENDER

Were that the distance between us
in the here and now
could vanish thus,
allowing these
rough hands that know
to explore these depths—just once.

Were that these arms could hold,
and these lips
mouth the untold.

Were that I could surrender,
to your grace and splendor.

# BARE

These words of mine,
imploring the stars to align,
so that you may shed all—
stand bare,
in your vulnerability,
all of you, right there.

So that I may catch your fall,
hold you, caress you,
press my lips against yours,
go down on all fours,
ride the waves with you
to the edge of insanity and back—

till we can no longer be consumed
by want's fire,
when we bask in desire.

# TWILIGHT

Broken,
Unshed tears,
Lonely twilight years,
Love's luster comes alive.
Survive.

# LOST

Lost,
Frightening, fading,
Twilight beckons bygones,
Living, missing out on
Life.

# WALLS

Those eyes—still seeking,
that heart—still anxious,
walled in to keep from breaking
from promises, half-baked and suspicious.

# DOES LOVE OPEN DOORS?

Maybe love isn't what opens the door—
perhaps it takes a lot, lot more.

# NEW DREAMS

For the first time,
in many years,
I've started dreaming again—

of the mountains we'd climb,
conquering our fears.
Your lover,
and now, your best friend.

And I'm jealous
of my words,
for they get to land
upon your eyes.

They get to be held,
to hear your lovely sighs.

They get to reach
your heart,
while I sit here,
oceans apart,

waiting for the day
I find a way—
for us never to part.

# CLEAR SPACE

I looked in the mirror
and couldn't find me.

Then a voice whispered in my ear,
"Let go of what holds you back,
and you will see."

# I LOVED, THEREFORE I LOST

I loved, therefore I lost—
my ego, my attitude—
and everything that I now know
came at a cost.

# INQUEST

Sometimes I wonder
if our need to love and be loved—
those hungers that rend
the very soul asunder—
were chains bestowed upon us
by the One above.

When petals grew heavy
upon the sepal's trust,
they were torn apart
by deeds, by words, by thoughts—unjust—
in the inquest
of a grief-stricken heart.

I tell twilight stories after sunset,
beneath veiled stars
that have never forgiven me.

And though I wrote my name in stardust,
they forgot—
for that which they do not know,
they cannot see.

# NOW YOU KNOW

Thank them
when they shatter your heart
into a million pieces.

Because now you know—
to love,
you don't need a million excuses.

# PAINTING STARS

I painted stars
in the darkest of hours,
and prayed their light
would hide my scars.

# BEHIND THAT SMILE

I see you,
hiding behind that smile,
tending to your fears
for a while,
afraid to fall
for someone else's guile.

# UPSETS

You're not holding onto upsets—
they're holding onto you.

Unfulfilled expectations, regrets,
and everybody else's points of view.

# FINDING YOU

I want to know you—
every inch of you.

I want to explore every mound,
every curve, every crevice,
your eyes, your lips,
your breasts—
and your tongue, too.

I want to make love to you
under the stars.
I want to caress
all your scars.

I want you to want me
as much as I do you—
every inch of me,
whenever you want me, too.

You're my goddess,
and I, a knave.
Bind me in chains,
and free this slave.

# FINDING ME

He knows how to bend
without breaking.
He knows how to heal
without taking.

He knows when to hold his tongue,
to offer kindness to hearts that are wrung.

He knows he must pave paths for the young,
not expecting to have his praises sung.

He knows failure is not a sin.
He has absorbed that feedback within.

He knows it's okay to be weak.
He knows when to let you speak.

He knows how to lend a listening ear.
He knows how to dispel your fear.

He knows it's okay to cry,
to let out a sigh.
He shines his light
when darkness is nigh.

And he knows
that the source of completeness
lies in his ability
to embrace forgiveness.

# SHEDDING SKIN

The demons that hide deep within
are released
with each layer of shedding skin.

The hurts and upsets we once took in,
when we were raw and mellow within.

And as each layer of what holds us back sheds,
we venture anew,
looking toward the road ahead.

# BUTS AND BECAUSE

If all you seek are flaws,
tucked neatly away
between those *buts* and *because*,
is it any wonder
that love is a lost cause?

# TRUST IS NOT THE ISSUE

It's not trust that's the issue—
it's about who shows up
when you're being *you*.

# WISDOM

You don't become mellow with age—
you just learn
how best to turn the page.

# CLOSURE

What if closure
is when you no longer feel
the need to forgive,
and accept that it's over?

# JOURNEY HOME

Someday, when we recall
all the places we did roam,
we will remember that all
we ever wanted
was to find our way back home.

And all it took
was for us
to unfetter our souls from guilt,
to release our *buts* and *because*,
and open the doors
to this home we built.

# WASTED CHANCES

That path we did not take,
fearing the unknown.
That phone call we didn't make,
for reasons all our own.

That call we did not answer,
to avoid conversations expected.
That message we didn't send her,
for fear of being rejected.

That plunge we thought a mistake,
too fearful of heights.
Those plans we had to forsake,
missing such wondrous sights.

That book we left unfinished,
assuming we knew how it ends.
Unexpressed feelings,
a spirit diminished,
by all that our ego rescinds.

Those words stuck deep in our throat,
begging to break free.
Every wasted chance
we wish we could smite,
to rebuild our destiny.

There are only so many seasons,
and second chances are rare.
Write down all those reasons—
it's that list that you must tear.

# EVOLVE

And as the battles rage around me,
I move to meet
the eye of the storm—

to pause a while,
to remember I was born free,
these scars define my very form.

This is who I am,
a reflection of courage,
quietly beautiful,
a mind unshaken,
a soul come of age.

Breaking the stigma of failure,
trusting the process,
rediscovering self-love's tender lure.

And every storm shall die,
and from its gentle eye
shall rise a snarl—
defiant, alive.

I'll let each frail wind rekindle
that spark that will not dwindle.

I have a choice,
to evolve, or remain;
to heed that voice
that whispers, *live not this life in vain.*

# THIS, TOO, IS LOVE

In these etched memories
where secrets unfold,
I crave to see stories
yet untold.

Demure poses I deem passion's art,
this sacred bond igniting my heart.
How do I know what remains unseen?
How do I tell her what I'm craving?

Like the fragrance of a flower,
inviting me to find what's left to discover.
Invoked by these visions of her,
desires begin to stir.

My thoughts are in disarray,
the sight of you holding me in sway.
Is it wrong to want more,
to ask—
*"Where were you before?"*

Do these palms ache to touch,
or would it be forbidden—too much?

Bound by promises to keep,
these images remain buried deep.
In the crevices of my mind,
this, too, is love—pure and kind.

# MEMORIES

# MEMORIES ON REWIND

The hallways of my mind
still whisper your name.
These arms,
where you were once entwined,
reach out for an embrace just the same.

Old photo albums reveal
hair strands that I find—
memoirs of a dying flame.
And I play memories on rewind,
to remember every fiber of your frame.

# DÉJÀ VU

I've walked that path before,
where I gave it my all,
until I could give no more—
and hung my memories on the wall.

# KINTSUGI

Sometimes, our broken
can't be mended,
if we hold on to it
like lost love's token,
long after it's ended.

And we can do better
the next time around,
when those pieces
we gather and mend whole.

And when it's time for us to be found,
they shall not find
a fractured soul.

# WORTHY

Was it that I was not worthy,
or is love truly that rare?

Did my sanity seem like madness,
or is it that you just didn't care?

# WHAT IFS

I recount memories of us in my head,
as I lay with the window open wide.
I toss and turn on this empty bed,
a constant reminder of a future denied.

# MONSOON MEMORIES

And there we were,
drenched by the heavy rain,
under the tree, in the narrow lane.

I watched you
as raindrops lingered on your lips.
I felt the brush of your fingertips.

And as you moved in closer,
your head on my shoulder, seeking shelter,
my heart pounded,
my tongue was tied,
my steady embrace—
my feelings belied.

These monsoon memories,
harbingers of untold stories.

And now,
when I feel the caress of the first rain,
I promise—
never to hold myself back again.

# THE ECHO

And though I promised to let go,
those words left unsaid
reverberate—
like an endless echo
in my head.

# SONGS WE USED TO SING

The radio reminds me
of the way we used to be,
when it plays the songs
we used to sing.

On those long drives,
when it was just you and me,
mouthing promises—
that we wouldn't change a thing.

# TO THE ONES THAT LED ME HERE

Here's to the ones who stayed,
and here's to the memories we made.

Here's to the dreams we let go,
and here's to those who helped us grow.

Here's to the ones we call home,
and here's to the ones we let roam.

Here's to burying the glories of the past,
and here's to building a future that lasts.

Here's to that ever-brimming cup,
and here's to never giving up.

# ORION

Do you still think of me
when you look up at the sky,
gazing at the stars
we used to see?

# HOW DO YOU REMEMBER ME?

How do you remember me?
Would I see,
in those misted eyes,
the wistful thoughts,
evoking smiles once more,
remnants of forgotten conversations
we've had before?

Were we guilty,
of driving wedges
between you and me,
with words left unspoken—
splinters of silence
that grew wider with time?

And when we could no longer find *us*,
had we simply lost
the will to seek?

# LEAVING BEHIND A PIECE OF ME

That laughter
sounds just like mine,
in the voice you strain to hear.

That shoulder you miss
when you're afraid,
or when you need to shed a tear.

Memories ignited
by the fragrance
of my favorite food,
a tinge of regret
whenever you hear
all those words misconstrued.

Can't you see?
In all these little things,
I've left behind
a piece of me.

# THE FINAL EMBRACE

It was our final embrace,
and I can still feel
her lips brush my face.

Her fragrance still lingers
where she rested her head
on my shoulders.

And I still look over my shoulder
when I hear laughter,
thinking it's her.

Was there no sound when my heart broke?
Could she hear me
when my silence spoke?

Did we fix it
when we picked up our pieces,
consoling ourselves,
calling it one of our hits and misses?

Sometimes, love is like a book left incomplete,
with dog-eared pages
we go back to read.

# SERENDIPITY

# ALMS

Will she run out of stories
to share with me someday?
When she is in my soul,
and I'm in hers,
and we don't need
to give anything away.

# SEE WHAT I SEE

Someday, maybe,
when the light in these eyes fades,
I hope you will see
that I saw our debt repaid.

That I laid my heart bare
and asked you to
find yourself there—
in a place that was safe, kind, and true.

Where we were spent
of reasons, *buts*, and *because*,
and all that was present
was our love, devoid of flaws.

And someday, you will see
the purity I said was true,
and all that had mattered to me
was to love and be loved by you.

# REST HERE

This shoulder
still waiting,
for her
to stop hesitating.

# AND HERE

Come,
rest on my shoulder,
forget your strife.
We've done navigating the map of life.

Close your eyes.
This is where our dreams
obliterate our weary sighs.

# SUMMER RAIN

Unfulfilled dreams, unmet desires,
all that our heart aspires,
all the heartache, all the pain,
cleansed by the summer rain.

# SKIN-DEEP

You would, perhaps,
think differently of me,
when you know
my demons within.

You would know me better,
if only you could see,
the words buried deep
beneath my skin.

# SHE IS ART

She is art,
broken pieces
beautifully pieced together.

On her sleeves, she wears her heart—
she has an embrace
for every stormy weather.

# YOUR PLAYLIST

Your playlist tells me who you are,
those songs you listen to,
they speak to me from afar.

# WHAT LIES AHEAD

I know we didn't speak a lot,
and yet we remember
all that was unsaid.

We embraced what is, and what is not,
what's behind us and what lies ahead.

# CRESTFALLEN

Crestfallen lovers,
open hearts, absent reasons,
shoulders broad and strong,
gentle arms, stretched wide open,
embracing lost love's seasons.

# THE LAST CHAPTER

It's only when we finish the last chapter
can we start reading books anew.
It's always the morning after
that bids the past adieu.

# ALCHEMY

# FINDING MY WAY TO YOU

I cannot decide
if it's your delicate shoulder,
bare,
or your hair,
that calls me closer,
like a dare,
to rest my head there.

Or perhaps it's your eyes,
mischievous, ever seekin,
the repressed sighs,
once betrayed, now misgiving,
still gracious,
silent, yet speaking,
telling me
you've been waiting
for me to find my way to you.

Is that what it means—
that the route to your soul
is what makes one whole?
And all that was written before
is wiped clean,
scarring no more.

# DISTANCE

On days like these,
I crave you.
And though we are separated by seas,
our hearts are enjoined, like glue.

# IN HER "ALMOST"

I love
the many ways
in which she says
she loves me.
And in her hesitant "almost,"
I hear how she loves me the most.

# I SEE YOU

I see you
in all the colors of the painted sky,
in the hues of orange and blue,
weaved into the fabric of the clouds
that pass by.

# FEWER REASONS

The more
you love for reasons few,
the more
the reasons
will open up for you.

# ON A FLIGHT TO NOWHERE

On a flight to nowhere,
I think of you,
and your gorgeous hair,
trussed over your shoulder,
your eyes, inviting me there.

Your smile, seeking answers,
your words, landing gently on me,
humbly requesting
that I make you see
how much you mean to me.

And here I am,
loving you like only I can.
With all my heart, with all my mind,
with all my soul,
plating these words of love,
beautifully decorating your heart's bowl.

So that you may partake
in this humble offering I make,
of words that will reverberate
in the chambers of your heart—
"I love you".

# DREAMS INTO MATTER

She holds my heart in her hand.
I hear her words before they land—
*"What sort of madness is this?"*

We laugh at our loss,
and weep at our bliss.

These few degrees of separation
between you
and these arms of mine
are mended
by the quiet reparation
of lost time—
two timeless souls
still seeking each other
through metaphors and rhyme.

Tinkering with destiny
to mend what it stole,
you and I,
we turn our dreams to matter,
setting them free.

# WHERE DO YOU GO?

I wonder what thoughts linger
in your head,
when you gaze through
those beautiful eyes,
and lie awake in bed.

I wonder which songs you play
to bring light to a tired soul,
and what quiet voices whisper
in the deep recesses
of your mind's control.

I wonder why those lips are pursed,
why those gentle fists are clenched,
is it your silent heart
calling out
to be healed,
to be nursed?

You are strong within,
even if you don't know it yet.
You are not alone,
lest you forget.

You carry the blessings
of every life you've touched,
and the strength
of all who love you
so much.

# CONVERSATIONS

'Twas a night like this,
a shy moon shrouded by a cloud,
just you and I, a lingering kiss.
It's lonely when two is a crowd.

And though we had it all, all was amiss.
Can you hear the silence?

It's loud.

# RENEWAL

Her wistful eyes spoke of desire,
seeking lost love's renewal.
She was fire—
and I,
her fuel.

Her warm touch on my head,
asking me to make her whole,
her coy smile.
as she lays on my bed,
calls out to my bereft soul.

The sun peeks through the blinds,
spying on us,
our worlds undone,
our tongues chasing
the taste
of what lust finds.

# JASMINES IN HER HAIR

I dreamt of fragrant flowers last night,
the kind we adorn deities with.
And I fantasized, recalling the sight
of a beautiful soul baring it all, bit by bit.

Did you dream of me, like I dreamt of you?
Did you feel all that I felt, too?

# UNSHAKEABLE BONDS

What people say about you
does not change
what I feel for you.

Do not let what they say about me
change it, too.

# NO MATTER WHAT

Give me your hand.
Let mine be the one that guides—
to protect,
to shield,
to be the one who provides.

I want to see you shine and thrive.
All you have to do
is take the dive.

Let me be the one you share with.
I'll be your sponge,
to soak up the weight
of your worries and care.
You already know
I'll always be there.

And someday,
when we've outgrown
the fear of feeling trapped or caught,
you'll see that troubled times
were never meant to last—
when a rock whispers,
"I'll be here,
no matter what."

# A REASON TO STAY

Maybe it was the way
your hair fell across your forehead,
or how your eyes would follow me
as I crossed the floor.
Maybe it was the magic we shared in bed,
not caring
what the mornings had in store.

Maybe it was the way
my heart skipped a beat
when your lips curved into a smile.
Maybe it was the way I felt complete
when your head rested on my shoulder
for a while.

Or maybe it was simply this—
that we never had to speak
to know what we had to say.

Just maybe,
we never had to seek
a reason to stay.

# YOU ARE INCREDIBLE

In a crowded room,
I will make you feel
like you're the only one around.
When I hold you close,
we will drown out the clutter and sound.

Do you see what I see?
Do you hear what I hear?
What we have been seeking is right here!

There are days that will come
that we wish they hadn't,
things we would've said or done
that we wish we didn't.
And when your heart sinks,
and I see those frowns,
I'll ensure those troubles
are drowned by your laughter's sounds.

It feels so right
when I hold you tight.
It feels like home
when I kiss your lips.
This is how I feel, my forever.
It doesn't matter where I am—
I'll always be here.

# MIDNIGHT MUSINGS

I wake up in the night,
wondering,
what thoughts flicker
behind those beautiful eyes,
as your dreams take flight.

Do you dream of us
like I do?
Do you hear
those voices too?
The ones that tell me
that I was made for you,
and you for me?

Do you see how
my love
lights up the path,
to show you the way
to me?

# SECRETS

To love is to dare,
to lay your secrets open
and bare.

# ALL OF THAT WHICH KEEPS ME WHOLE

A beautiful mind,
an old soul,
a clear heart,
no desire to control.

A listening ear,
eyes on the goal,
inherent grace,
that fills every hole.

Feet on the ground,
hands to fill that bowl,
are all the parts
that keep you whole.

# BRIGHTER DAYS

And suddenly, the days seem brighter,
and the nights don't seem too long.
The heart seems to grow lighter,
and the soul, strong.

When kindred souls meet
along this lonely pathway,
there's someone to share with and greet.
And then,
what troubles us will be driven away.

# MELODY

I cannot begin to describe how I rejoice,
when I hear the sound of your voice.
Gentle, harmonious, and calm,
like a soft caress across my palm.

I feel a thrill as my fingertips
linger over that mark on your lips.
And as your lips curve into a smile,
I know, together,
we've walked another mile.

# THAT'S YOUR HOME

When you don't have to say it,
and yet you are heard.
When harmony is transcended,
and the soul nurtured.

When you feel loved,
even when you're not being held.
It matters not where you roam—
that's your home.

# SILENT TEARS

You shed a silent tear,
and I am so far away.
I wish you could rest your head here
at the end of a trying day.

# WHEN THOSE MOMENTS COME

There are moments every day
when dread leads our thoughts astray.
And when it all feels overwhelming,
I'll be there when those moments come.

If nightmares seem any scarier,
stand behind me—I'll be the barrier.
Your cheerleader, your rock,
stand by my side, and see what I see—
it's not much further, this walk.

Turn the corner, hold my hand,
release the anchor.
When you see where the light comes from,
I'll be there when those moments come.

# I'LL BE WAITING HERE

It matters not how far you wander,
or what you seek.
It matters not what lies yonder,
or if at the future you cannot peek.

When that path finally appears,
you will find me—patiently waiting here.

# UNSEEN. UNSPOKEN.
# UNOPENED. UNCHISELED

What dreams simmer beneath those lovely eyes,
still bright despite deception and lies?

What words remain unspoken behind that shy smile,
weary from a journey yet to see its last mile?

What fears hold back that beautiful heart,
from opening up again, lest sanity may dart?

Only the sculptor knows what lies beneath that rock—
beautiful art, that only his chisel can unlock.

# SHACKLED HEART

When you set yourself free
from your shackled heart,
come to me.
I'll tear those demons apart,
the ones that won't let you be.
'Tis a strong hand that can part those fetters.
This is the way—can't you see?

Free yourself when you find yourself here,
free your heart from shackles,
chained by demons of doubt and fear,
nibbled at by jackals.
Free yourself from the past you hold dear.

# NO EXCUSES

I will not offer excuses,
as an apology for life's bruises.

I offer your soul,
promises,
to make you whole.

# I WOULD HAVE

If I could have loved you
in a million different ways,
I would have.

If my words didn't
set your heart ablaze,
they should have.

# WASTING SUNSETS OVER REGRETS

Cover me in sunrise,
before you say your goodbyes.
Just you and I, and our thoughts,
no judges, no juries calling the shots.

One foot in front of the other,
mind devoid of clutter.
Why waste our sunsets…
over regrets?

# SOLACE

Someday, our journey home
will be paved with flowers,
and the million thoughts that roam
will find solace under these bowers.

# BEFORE WE SLEEP

Before we sleep,
may we find
a moment to mend,
to have our hearts realigned.

Before we plant
that goodnight kiss,
may we find forgiveness
and leave nothing amiss.

And before our dreams
weave their silken thread,
may we not
leave words unsaid.

And when we touch,
may we keep
ourselves
in quietude's tender clutch.

In those moments
before we slip
into deep slumber,
may the love we feel
be much, too much.

# LOVE'S EMBRACE

May these words find you,
nestled in love's gentle hue.
May these hours in between
my missing you and you waking,
be filled with knowing
that you will be nestled in strong arms.
Cherishing you with forever's embrace,
through those times
when moments are long,
and we pine to see each other's face.

# ABOUT THE AUTHOR

Kalpesh Desai is a serial tech entrepreneur who turns to poetry as a way to process his thoughts, breakthroughs, and human reflections drawn from decades of leadership and reinvention.

A management graduate from one of India's foremost business schools, Kalpesh has spent over 3 decades building and leading technology enterprises across financial services, insurance, manufacturing, retail, distribution, and oil & gas. He was named among the *Top 10 Financial Technology CEOs of 2020* by *CEO Insight* and was featured in *INSEAD's* case study on *3i Infotech*, which showcased his pioneering go-to-market strategy that drove the company's organic growth.

He leads **Agile Financial Technologies** as its President and CEO, and holds multiple board and advisory positions across industries, including retail, manufacturing, investment banking, and technology.

amazon.com/author/kalpeshpdesai
instagram.com/kalpeshdesai.official
linkedin.com/in/kalpeshdesai